Nutmeg Gets A Little Sister

Written by Judith Foxon

Illustrated by Sarah Rawlings

Note about the author

Judith Foxon is an adoption worker at the Catholic Children's Society, Nottingham. She is married, with three daughters, two by birth and one who joined them at the age of eight, bringing joy to the family and fuelling Judith's interest in the adoption of older children. The family also brought up a foster daughter, who suffers from ADHD. Judith has many years of experience in preparing families for children of all ages and direct work with children has formed a significant part of her work. Her post-adoption work with children, teenagers and young adults regularly covers issues of loss and contact. Along with the popular "Nutmeg" series, she is also the author of *Spark Learns to Fly*, all published by BAAF.

Note about the illustrator

The illustrations in this book have been drawn by Sarah Rawlings. Sarah has also illustrated *Nutmeg Gets Adopted, Nutmeg Gets Cross, Nutmeg Gets a Letter, Nutmeg Gets a Little Help* and *Nutmeg Gets into Trouble*, and another series of books to use with children, also published by BAAF. Titles include: *Feeling Safe, Living with a New Family* and *Hoping for the Best*.

Sarah's illustrations in the Nutmeg series were inspired by originals first drawn by Jessica, a young friend of the author's. Herself adopted, Jessica helped bring the project to life with her charming and colourful illustrations when the project was first piloted. She shared her original illustrations and the ideas behind them with Sarah.

Acknowledgements

Integrating a new child into the family can be a tricky business initially but in most families things settle down fairly quickly. However, as I began to write the guidelines for *Nutmeg Gets a Little Sister* and reflected on the families I know who have adopted birth siblings – whether placed at the same time or sequentially – or adopted an unrelated child, and considered the problems parents and children are grappling with (or have overcome), I realised yet again how much they have taught me. Nutmeg is a composite of many of the children I know. I am privileged to work closely with families for only a short time but I hold them in my heart for much longer. I owe them a great deal and would like to say a heartfelt 'Thank you'. I would also like to thank my friends and colleagues at the Catholic Children's Society, Nottingham for their encouragement. Finally I would like to thank Shaila Shah, Jo Francis and Hedi Argent and the rest of the team at BAAF for their unfailing help and support and, of course, Sarah Rawlings, whose drawings bring Nutmeg's stories to life. I believe in adoption and feel a lucky woman that Nutmeg has helped some children and families understand and enjoy their adoption experience a little better.

Judith Foxon
June 2007

Nutmeg, Poppy and Hops are three little squirrels who live with their adopted mummy and daddy in a nest in a big oak tree. Nutmeg and Poppy hurry home from school, running along branches and jumping from one tree to another. Nutmeg is carrying Hops on his back.

When they get home, Mummy Fern gives Nutmeg, Poppy and Hops a big hug and brushes their fur while they tell her about their day at school. She gives them some yummy blackberry tarts. When they're sitting around the table, Mummy Fern says, "I had a letter from your birth mummy Holly today."

Nutmeg doesn't see Mummy Holly but every year Mummy Fern sends her a letter telling Holly good things about Nutmeg, Poppy and Hops, and Mummy Holly writes back. Nutmeg likes to know she's OK.

Last year, when she wrote to say she had a new baby squirrel called Pip, Nutmeg's tummy felt very funny. If Mummy Holly couldn't keep him and Poppy and Hops safe, what about Pip? Would Pip get hurt? If Mummy Holly could look after Pip safely, why couldn't she look after them? Nutmeg had felt very confused and got cross and cried. Mummy Fern had rocked him like a baby to make him feel better.

Today, Mummy Fern told Nutmeg, Poppy and Hops that Mummy Holly and Pip's dad couldn't keep Pip safe. She had fallen out of the tree and broken her tail. Her tail was mended now but she was going to be adopted. Nutmeg and Poppy shouted together, "Can she come and live with us, Mummy? Please!" "She can share my room," said Poppy.

A social worker came to visit the family lots of times. He asked Nutmeg, Poppy and Hops how they would feel if Mummy Fern and Daddy Foxglove spent a lot of time looking after Pip.

He asked Nutmeg how he would feel if Pip broke his new cricket bat and what Poppy would feel if Pip scribbled all over her books. They said they wouldn't mind and Hops said he would be glad not to be the littlest any more.

Nutmeg felt a bit worried about Pip coming to live with them because when he was living in his birth family he had to look after Poppy and Hops. He had to find acorn biscuits for breakfast and mix chestnut milk in a bottle for baby Hops.

Nutmeg didn't want to look after Pip. But he remembered that Mummy Fern never left her little squirrels to get their own breakfast and he felt better.

Then the social worker told Nutmeg, Poppy and Hops that Pip could come and live with them. They were very excited and sorted out some of their toys for her to play with.

Nutmeg was excited and worried at the same time. What if she doesn't like us? What if we don't like her? They visited Pip many times and, once she got used to them, she came to live with them in the big oak tree.

At first it was fun to have a little sister and Nutmeg, Poppy and Hops would argue about whose turn it was to play with her. Poppy loved her brothers but it was nice to have another girl in the family.

Some days were difficult because Pip missed Mummy Holly and would cry. Nutmeg and Poppy thought she didn't like them but Mummy Fern said it was OK because Pip could love them and miss Mummy Holly at the same time.

Having someone as little as Pip in the family made Hops feel very grown up and he liked it. But sometimes, when he went to school and Pip stayed home with Mum, Hops felt jealous.

Pip was happy having
Mum to herself and sometimes when
Nutmeg, Poppy and Hops came home from school,
she was grumpy and would shout and stamp her feet.

Once, Pip spilt a jar of water all over Poppy's picture and Poppy shouted at her. When Mummy Fern told Poppy not to shout at Pip, Poppy burst into tears.

Mummy Fern hugged her and said it was an accident. Then Pip came and said "Sorry," and Poppy gave her a hug.

Looking at the pictures in Pip's life story book brought back some sad memories for Nutmeg and Poppy. Hops asked lots of questions because he couldn't remember living with Mummy Holly and Daddy Ginger.

After a while everyone settled down together. Nutmeg, Poppy and Hops would take turns playing bubbles with Pip when she had her bath and Pip loved to sit on their knees while they read her stories. If they were climbing trees they had to take turns looking after Pip because she was too little to climb very high.

Pip's social worker came to see them and asked Nutmeg, Poppy and Hops what it felt like to have Pip in the family – what was nice and what wasn't.

Pip's social worker said Nutmeg, Poppy and Hops were kind little squirrels to share their mummy and daddy with Pip. They told him that though they felt jealous sometimes, they loved Pip and were glad she'd joined their family.

One night, after Pip had gone to bed, Mummy Fern and Daddy Foxglove asked Nutmeg, Poppy and Hops if they wanted Pip to stay with them for always. They all said "Yes."

Daddy Foxglove said that he and Mummy were going to write to the Wise Owl judge and say they wanted to adopt Pip.

In the morning, Mummy Fern read Pip a story about a little squirrel who was going to be adopted. Pip said, "Stay here. No move." Mummy Fern gave her a big hug and said, "We all love you, Pip, and you can stay with us for always." Pip gave Mummy Fern a big hug.

After school, Daddy Foxglove asked Nutmeg, Poppy and Hops if they wanted to draw a picture or write a letter to the Wise Owl. Nutmeg wrote, "Dear Wise Owl, Pip is my little sister and I love her. I want her to stay with our family. Love, Nutmeg."

Poppy wrote, "Dear Wise Owl, Mummy Fern and Daddy Foxglove are the best mum and dad in the world and will take good care of Pip. I love having a little sister. Poppy xx." Hops drew a picture of the whole family with him holding Pip's hand.

The next time Pip's social worker came, he brought a Wise Owl puppet. He said, "Let's pretend I'm Wise Owl, the judge." Then he asked Mummy and Daddy, "Why do you want to adopt Pip?" Daddy Foxglove said, "Because we love her and want to be her mummy and daddy forever." Mummy Fern said, "Because our children Nutmeg, Poppy and Hops love Pip and want her to be their sister."

"Will you be kind to Pip, play with her and keep her safe?" asked Wise Owl. "Yes," they said, and Pip jumped up and down and made everyone laugh.

Not long afterwards, everyone put on their best clothes and went to see the real Wise Owl. Daddy Foxglove carried Pip because she was feeling a bit anxious. Poppy and Hops held Mummy Fern's hand and Nutmeg held Daddy's hand.

The Wise Owl judge was very friendly. He said Pip looked happy in her new family and he was glad she had such a loving sister and brothers as Nutmeg, Poppy and Hops. He let them watch while he signed the adoption order, which meant Pip could stay with them for always.

Then Pip's social worker took a photo of everyone standing next to the judge. After that they said thank you and waved goodbye to the Wise Owl.

In the afternoon, all their friends came around to the nest in the oak tree and Mummy Fern, Daddy Foxglove, Nutmeg, Poppy, Hops and Pip had the biggest adoption party! Pip was part of their family forever!

Nutmeg Gets A Little Sister
PRACTICE GUIDELINES

By Judith Foxon with Hedi Argent

Published by
British Association for Adoption & Fostering
(BAAF)
Saffron House
6–10 Kirby Street
London EC1N 8TS
www.baaf.org.uk

Charity registration 275689

© Judith Foxon, 2007
Illustrations © Sarah Rawlings, 2007
Reprinted 2009, 2010, 2012

British Library Cataloguing in Publication Data
A catalogue record for this book is available from the British Library

ISBN 978 1 905664 22 1

Guidelines written by Judith Foxon
Edited by Hedi Argent
Project management by Jo Francis, BAAF
Designed and typeset by Nick Rawlings
Printed in Great Britain The Lavenham Press Ltd
Trade distribution by Turnaround Publisher Services, Unit 3, Olympia Trading Estate, Coburg Road, London N22 6TZ

All rights reserved. Apart from any fair dealing for the purposes of research or private study, or criticism or review, as permitted under the Copyright, Designs and Patents Act 1988, this publication may not be reproduced, stored in a retrieval system, or transmitted in any form or by any means, without the prior written permission of the publishers.

The moral right of the author has been asserted in accordance with the Copyright, Designs and Patents Act 1988.

BAAF is the leading UK-wide membership organisation for all those concerned with adoption, fostering and child care issues.

Introduction

WHY ARE SIBLINGS IMPORTANT?
Our sibling relationships are often the longest of our lives. They can be close, they can be fun, supportive or definitely prickly depending on the personalities and life experiences of the individuals concerned, and they shape our vision of who we are. We are all strongly affected by the way family members see us, and our sisters and brothers offer us a life-long yardstick whereby we may measure ourselves.

WHY DO WE HAVE DIFFERENT EXPERIENCES OF OUR BIRTH FAMILY?
Each person's experience of family is unique and even sisters and brothers who have grown up together will experience family life differently. The way our parents love us and the manner in which they express it will not be the same for all of their children. As parents we "practise" on our children, so the first child sometimes has a more difficult passage to adulthood and independence because they are a "trailblazer" for subsequent siblings.

It is said that the qualities we dislike in ourselves irritate us even more when we find them in other people. Whilst enjoying a particularly close relationship with the child whose personality most resembles our own, we may often clash with them and the child may have an easier relationship with their other parent. We may also expect higher standards from the child who is most like us. We may treat boys and girls differently and be more patient with the little girl who cries when she's upset (or to get her own way) than we are with her brother.

ARE PARENTS INFLUENCED BY THEIR OWN UPBRINGING?
We are all affected by the parenting we have received. We may consciously try to copy what our parents did for us or react against it; we all have a "role model" somewhere in our unconscious that shapes our behaviour with our own children. How many of us, in response to the umpteenth 'Why?', instinctively respond with 'Because I said so!', despite our best intentions?

The need to reflect on the way we parent, and why, is important and perhaps the most tiring part of our job!

Many neglected and abused children grow up to be good and thoughtful parents. But parents of children who live in neglectful and abusing families may have experienced abuse in their own childhood, and are more likely to parent instinctively rather than reflectively. So the woman who was sexually abused as a child may accept the same for the daughter who looks like her. The mother who was abused by her father and brothers may abuse her son and favour her daughter or unload the emotional abuse she suffered as a child onto the son who resembles her, whilst nurturing her other children. A stepfather who was the rejected oldest son in his own family may find it difficult to like or care for his older stepson. If he is separated from his own children, he may resent a stepson who is the same age as his estranged birth son – or be attracted to him. A child may resent another man taking over from his absent birth father or being replaced himself as the "man" in the family. However, a younger brother may welcome the same man and enjoy a really positive relationship with his stepfather.

After his father left, Ian was the "man" of the family until his mother remarried. He resented his stepfather, and the dislike was mutual. Ian's sister, Clare, had never known her birth father and loved her stepfather, which caused friction between the siblings which persisted into adult life.

There are so many variables in family life that it's not surprising that each child experiences it differently, and these experiences will affect the way they feel about and respond to each other.

SIBLING RELATIONSHIPS

Sibling relationships are emphasised when children are brought up in a "feral" way with little parental involvement. In this situation, sibling relationships will be particularly important and may depend on the child's place in the family "pecking order", whom they resemble, their physique, their quickness of wit, their defence mechanisms or their resilience. All of these factors will have a bearing on how a particular child gets on with each brother and sister and the alliances and rivalries that are established. Very often an older child assumes responsibility for younger siblings and may need to be given other "caring" responsibilities in their foster or adoptive family before they can "let go".

Liam was the eldest son of sexually abusing parents and took out his anger on his younger siblings by abusing them. A younger brother, Sean, had an inbuilt sense of "fair play" and tried to defend his younger siblings. Seven years on, Liam is still not able to have contact with his siblings because he is seen as potentially dangerous whilst Sean was able to be placed with a younger brother and enjoys regular contact with his other siblings.

WHY DO WE PLACE SIBLINGS TOGETHER OR APART?

As social workers and carers, we are very aware of the loss suffered by children who are removed from their birth family. It is therefore natural and commendable that we try to reduce the impact of their loss by keeping siblings together whenever possible. However, we need to assess these relationships carefully. They may be attached to each other, but is their attachment healthy? When siblings have had some of their emotional needs met within their birth family – like Nutmeg, Poppy and Hops – being placed together allows the children to draw strength and support from each other as well as from their foster or adoptive families. In this case, once they have formed secure attachments to their new parents, the children (or squirrels!) may be able to welcome a new child into their family.

The incoming child will arouse memories and feelings in the established children which are connected with their own past but, with sensitivity on the part of the adults around them, the family can generally settle down with little more than the usual jealousies. The "attention balance" shifts but, like a mobile, which trembles when a new figure is added, it reforms into a new and stable shape.

For the first three years of her life, Lara was a much loved daughter and youngest sister. Then, shortly after her father left, her mother died and the family was scattered. Between the ages of four and eight, Lara had several moves and some very difficult experiences. At eight she was placed in an adoptive family with two existing birth children. Lara retained contact with two of her older siblings and her grandmother. These relationships were a big factor in the success of her adoption, but another was Lara's non-confrontational personality.

When children come from a birth family where their emotional needs remained largely unmet, the situation is more complex. The child's paramount need is to attach securely to a parent who can provide safety, stability and love. Until this is achieved, some children may compete for their parents' attention in ways that will sabotage their sibling's attempts to form a healthy attachment. Only when children are able to form healthy and happy attachments to new parents will they be able to reach out to a sibling in a positive rather then a competitive way. Before children are placed together in a permanent family, it is important that their separate attachment patterns are assessed and understood. The prospective carer's style of parenting – secure, dismissive, anxious, etc – should also be assessed because this will affect their ability to meet the individual needs of different children.

Initially, most very young children enjoy being around other children, but they do not play *with* them, they play *alongside* them. It takes a while to develop the skills for reciprocal play and sharing. When children have had to "watch out for themselves", they often haven't learnt these skills, and therefore placing two such siblings together can be fraught as the new carers' attempts to respond to one child are sabotaged by the other child's desperate efforts to gain attention.

Flo had experienced several failed attempts to rehabilitate her with her birth mother. Her younger sister experienced a secure foster home. When placed together, Flo was desperate to claim her adoptive parents but her "naughty" behaviour wasn't understood as grieving. Although she settled superficially, her grief resurfaced in her teens in a self-destructive pattern of running away so that her adoptive mother would come looking for her and claim her. Flo's younger sister had a smoother passage to adulthood.

WHAT DO WE NEED TO LOOK FOR?
When looking at whether siblings should be placed together, we need to observe and assess their relationship. Is it positive? Do they enjoy being together? Do they miss each other when they're apart? Is their rivalry within the usual range for children of their age? Do they protect, comfort and help each other? These are really positive signs.

Other observations are more worrying. Is one child constantly put down by the other? Does one child dominate the others? Is a child aggressive towards one particular sibling? Has any sexualised play between them been acknowledged and dealt with? Are they safe together? Do they try to disrupt the time their sibling spends with their carer? Meeting the extra needs of children from the care system can be challenging and many adoptive and foster carers struggle to meet the different needs of children placed together if one actively undermines positive experiences for their siblings. Whether this is deliberate or unconscious makes no difference to the effect on family life of extreme jealousy and competition for attention.

One of the most difficult things adoptive families have to contend with is the amount of anger an angry child can generate in the family as a whole. Most adopters and foster carers understand *why* a child may be angry but living with that anger without getting caught up in it can be very difficult. It is hard to help other children in the family understand what's happening and there is a real danger that an "acting out" child will take centre stage in the family – often for years – to the detriment of their quieter siblings. Thought should be given as to whether such a child might benefit from having a family to themselves.

Another difficult issue is where a child is actively and loudly dealing with issues from the past. Even if this is appropriate for them, it may be detrimental to a sibling who isn't ready to revisit the past. Where children have been placed together this difficulty needs to be managed, but if it is clearly present before placement it should be part of the equation when considering whether siblings should be placed together.

In a family with four children, the eldest child suffered from autism. His parents couldn't cope and locked him in the bedroom for large parts of the day. When a younger son was born, he also spent large parts of the day locked in with his brother. He was physically smaller, and his instinctive defence was to flee, but he couldn't escape. He tried to appease his brother but got punched, scratched and bitten on a regular basis. His fear of his older brother was such that when they were taken into care, the two boys could not be placed together. Even contact with his brother was an ordeal for the younger child. Placed alone, this boy's gentle nature was allowed to flourish. In contrast, a third brother, also subjected to bullying by the eldest, was a fighter by nature. Although cowed by his sibling and too frightened to want any contact with him, his fight defence reasserted itself in his adoptive home and he reacted to every stress with aggression. This caused problems when he was placed with his younger sister.

In another very large family, the birth parents physically and sexually abused their children. The older ones looked after their younger siblings at night; they slept on mattresses on the floor and cuddled up to each other to find security and comfort in physical closeness. However, while they were abused and during their waking hours it was every child for themselves. When they were assessed, it was found that four of the older children relied solely on themselves to get their needs met. They didn't trust their parents or each other. Because their experience had taught them to compete to get their own needs met, the rivalry between these siblings placed together in a foster or adoptive home would have prevented them from beginning to form more healthy relationships.

Placed separately, Eleanor, now 12, has a strong bond with her adoptive parents. She gets news of her brothers and sisters through her adoptive parents who keep in touch with the other adopters and sees one sister regularly and the others occasionally. Her "mind map" of family includes her adoptive family and siblings, although her priority attachment is to her adoptive parents.

Children may also need to be placed separately if they have abused each other within their birth family; the abusive relationship – whether sexual, physical or emotional – may persist or resurface in their foster or adoptive family. Sometimes even the memory of shared abuse can act as a permanent trigger and interfere with children forming new and secure attachments to their new parents.

A little girl of three was abused in foster care by her older brothers who, at that stage of their lives, closely identified with their abusive father. She needed to be placed in a separate adoptive home, where she thrived.

A young brother and sister persisted in trying to push things up each other's bottoms, and the younger acted this scenario out with glove puppets and hosepipes! Fortunately, they were placed with skilled adopters who were able to keep the children safe and work with them to help them overcome lessons learnt in their birth family.

Many of the above concerns apply equally to non-related children, since they may transfer their feelings for their siblings onto their adoptive brothers and sisters.

HOW IMPORTANT IS SIBLING CONTACT?

Direct contact is usually desirable if sisters and brothers are not living together. As each child becomes more confident and secure in family placement, sibling relationships should be enhanced. However, some children may need to reach a greater understanding of their past before they can benefit from seeing their siblings.

Often sibling contact is about the children having fun together, but in situations like the one below, it may be beneficial to have a meeting of siblings, carers and therapeutic social workers, when issues from the past can be discussed frankly. This can help children to move on and let go of some of the guilt they hold for what happened in the past. Such a meeting needs to be arranged and managed by people skilled in working with abuse as well as in adoption, and should be preceded by individual work with each child and preparation of the carers.

One child of eight placed in an adoptive family separately from abusive siblings had supervised contact with her brothers in a safe environment. However, all the feelings around the abuse got in the way. The boys felt guilty and their sister experienced contact itself as abusive. All the children had to work separately on their life stories before they could rebuild more normal sibling relationships. This required skilled post-adoption support from therapeutic social workers.

Siblings placed together sometimes have different contact arrangements with birth family members and this can be difficult to manage as children get older. Children from different families placed together are even more likely to have different contact arrangements, which can be unsettling. In many instances, as with the family above, all parties involved in post-adoption contact need ongoing support.

When her father left home, Anna's mother treated her young daughter as a confidante. Subsequently, her mother had two sons by a violent man who abused all three children. The boys bore the brunt of the abuse and were angry with their mother for not defending them. The three children were placed together in an adoptive family where Anna continued to see her birth mother twice a year. Her brothers didn't want any contact with their mother and didn't want Anna to share her experiences after contact, which angered her. The differing needs of the children caused tension in the family and when the children reached adolescence the situation became critical for a while. Fortunately, post-adoption support was available and the adoptive parents and children were able to make good use of it and are still together.

ISSUES ARISING WHEN A NEW SIBLING JOINS THE FAMILY

When Pip joins the family, Mummy Fern and Daddy Foxglove will not only be dealing with Pip's needs but also with the feelings her arrival will arouse in their established children. The fact that she is no longer at home with Mummy Holly may make her older siblings feel less "replaced". They may feel less disintegrated as a family now that Pip is with them. However, the thought of Pip's arrival reminds Nutmeg of how he looked after Poppy and Hops in their birth family and he doesn't want to have to look after Pip. Even though he knows Mummy Fern will do it all, there will be times when a simple request to 'Make sure Pip doesn't fall off that branch' may trigger memories of looking after Hops and the resentment associated with it.

Pip's life story book revives memories and feelings for Nutmeg and Poppy and leads Hops to start exploring his own past for the first time. Nutmeg and Poppy may have different questions and concerns about their experiences with Mummy Holly and Daddy Ginger now they are older. They may feel jealous that Pip lived with her more recently than they have. Pip's arrival may bring Mummy Holly into their adoptive family in a real way, and Mummy Fern may be treated as Mummy Holly from time to time even by her older children, while Daddy Foxglove might be treated like Daddy Ginger or Pip's birth father. As Pip grows old enough to share her experiences of Mummy Holly, it may confirm Nutmeg's own memories and strengthen his understanding of why he was adopted or lead him to question it again. Pip's life story book may lead into a discussion about siblings having different fathers, as is often true for siblings placed sequentially.

Although feelings of jealousy are normal when a new child arrives in an emotionally healthy birth family, they can be more troubling for children whose primary attachments are still developing. However, sensitive parenting will help the children to come through not only unscathed but stronger. Helping to care for a younger sibling can develop a sense of pride and self-confidence in a child and offer them the nurturing opportunity to "revisit" their infancy by playing with bottles, nappies and toys designed for a younger age group.

PREPARING CHILDREN FOR THE ADOPTION HEARING

Before children are placed for adoption, we try to help them understand why they have had to leave their birth family and why they will have a new family to look after them. When they have been placed for adoption, we encourage them to develop a sense of family that integrates their birth and adoptive families, by making family trees and lighting candles or drawing hearts for everyone they love.

Before Looked After Children (LAC) reviews we support children to complete their own child-friendly review form, which asks questions such as: 'What makes you happy in your adoptive family?'; 'When do you feel sad?'; 'Who do you tell your worries to?'; 'Who do you think of from the past?'; 'Who do you talk to about sad memories?' and 'Who do you share happy memories with?'

Before the adoption papers are lodged in the court, we check again that the child understands why they have left their birth family – perhaps with a story like *Spark Learns to Fly* – and explain the next stage of their adoption journey – perhaps with *Nutmeg Gets Adopted*.

Older children may like to see their original birth certificate and most children can be involved in helping their adopters to fill out the section of the application form stating their proposed name. Children need to be reassured that the judge will not randomly remove them from their adoptive family and that their social worker will be telling the judge what a good idea it is for them to be adopted. Many children like to write their own letter to the judge or to draw a picture of themselves in their adoptive family.

Children can be reassured by playing out a brief adoption scenario with glove puppets or something similar. The "judge" can ask questions like 'Mummy Fern, you will keep little Pip safe and never smack her?', to which Mummy Fern can respond reassuringly. Parents can be invited to say how much they love their adopted child, and children can feel more in control when they play the judge. This game should be a lot of fun and can be played over and over again by the family at home.

Some courts allow prospective adopters to take their children to see the place where they will meet the judge. Anything that helps children to enjoy the adoption hearing will also help them to remember it as a day for celebration. BAAF publishes booklets for young children that explain the whole process called *What Happens in Court?* and *Adoption: What it is and what it means*.

Judith Foxon
June 2007

Guide to the text

Setting the scene

If children are familiar with some of the earlier Nutmeg stories, it is a good idea to talk over what they and you remember about them.

Why were Nutmeg, Poppy and Hops adopted?

What happened when they came to live with Mummy Fern and Daddy Foxglove?

Who is their birth mother?

Which story do you like best?

Do you think Nutmeg is a bigger squirrel now?

Children like to be reminded of what they know; it confirms their view of the world.

Reading this book with adopted children offers opportunities for a range of discussions appropriate to age and understanding. The following comments and questions are merely suggestions about how to use the text and should be amended to fit the circumstances of individual children.

PAGES 1-2 Emotional subjects

Playing on the way back from school and having a treat when they get home are reassuring routines for most children. Telling what they have done at school can be more difficult because many children tend to keep friends, school and family in different compartments in their minds. It is not unusual for a child to say 'I don't know' or 'I can't remember', when asked anything about the school day.

If you're not a squirrel, what games can you play on the way home from school?

Nutmeg, Poppy and Hops tell Mummy Fern all about their day at school. Is it easy to talk about school when you get home?

The letter from Mummy Holly is introduced when the young squirrels are sitting comfortably around the table. It is important to wait until children are relaxed, not hungry or tired, before broaching emotional subjects.

PAGE 3 Letterbox contact

Letterbox contact has become the most usual way for adopted children to maintain their connection with their birth families. If managed with good will by the adopters, if there is openness in the adoptive family and if the birth family is adequately supported to sustain the exchange of information, then letterbox contact can enable children to keep absent people in mind while leaving the door open for other forms of contact later on. Perhaps Mummy Fern saves all Mummy Holly's letters in a special folder so that the young squirrels can look at them whenever they want to, or maybe Mummy Fern will look after the letters until her children are older.

Nutmeg's anxieties about his new baby sister are shared by many children in this situation.

What kind of things does Mummy Fern write to Mummy Holly?

Do you think they should send photos to each other?

Could Nutmeg, Poppy and Hops send anything to Mummy Holly?

Why did Nutmeg's tummy feel funny? What bothers him?

PAGE 4 News from the birth family

The bad news about Pip raises Nutmeg's anxiety about his baby sister but also validates his own bad memories.

Children are inevitably jealous of siblings who remain with their birth parents. The unspoken questions are always 'What did I do? What is wrong with me? Why didn't she want me?' Rescuing Pip is easier than dealing with these complicated feelings. But some children may have to accept the painful fact that their sibling will not be able to join them.

It is important to note that Pip is Nutmeg's half-sister because Daddy Ginger is not her birth father.

PAGE 5 Being chosen

It is reassuring to remind children that their adoptive family was specially chosen for them. Mummy Fern and Daddy Foxglove now have to be specially chosen for Pip. The views and needs of Nutmeg, Poppy and Hops also have to be taken seriously.

Do you remember your social worker? What was their name?

PAGES 6-8 Waiting for Pip

There are mixed feelings while assessments and decisions are made about adding a new child to the family. It is natural for Nutmeg to be both excited and apprehensive. Children should be enabled to express their fears as well as their hopes. Living with a baby sister is not quite the same as thinking about it.

Is Nutmeg right to worry about having to look after Pip?

Do you know the story about Hops falling out of the nest?

Daddy Ginger isn't Pip's father – who is? What do you think happened to Daddy Ginger?

Does Nutmeg feel jealous of Pip? What makes you feel jealous?

Why do Nutmeg, Poppy and Hops want Pip to come and live with them?

What might happen to Pip if she can't come to live with Mummy Fern and Daddy Foxglove?

Why do you think the social worker chose Mummy Fern and Daddy Foxglove to be the squirrels' mummy and daddy?

Is there anything Nutmeg, Poppy and Hops should ask the social worker?

Can you be excited and pleased and worried all at the same time?

Why did Pip make several visits before she moved in?

What would be the best thing about having a baby sister? What would be the worst?

NUTMEG GETS A LITTLE SISTER: PRACTICE GUIDELINES

PAGES 9-12 New family relationships

It is very distressing to watch a grieving infant and it is hard for the other young squirrels to understand that Pip's misery has nothing to do with them. Children quickly feel it's their fault if they think something is wrong. In this situation all the children need extra hugs and attention.

Every new addition to a family changes existing relationships. Hops feels more grown up but has lost his place as the youngest; Poppy has a sister to share her room but she is no longer the only girl; Nutmeg is proud of his baby sister but as the eldest he may be expected to be more responsible than he always wants to be.

Why is Pip crying? Will she get used to her new family?

Does Hops like having a younger brother?

What can you do when a baby spoils your games?

Will Mummy Fern be too busy to play with Nutmeg now?

Are you the youngest, oldest, or in the middle in your family?

PAGE 13 Life story books

Life story work is neverending. It should help adopted children to put their two families together and to experience continuity in their lives. Life story books are just one way of doing this. When Nutmeg was younger, he got muddled about being adopted and a social worker came to help him (*Nutmeg Gets a Little Help*). Nutmeg, Poppy and Hops have their own life story books and Mummy Fern and Daddy Foxglove help them to keep adding to their stories and to talk about them whenever they want to.

It is important not to treat life story books as precious objects to be put away and taken out on special occasions. Children may not want to look at their books at one stage, and be preoccupied with their own story at other times.

One child of seven kept her life story book under her bed for two years and never wanted to look at it. Then one day it appeared on her bedside table and she asked her mother to read it with her every night for a month. At the end of the month, a bit worse for wear, it went back under the bed.

Can you remember the good things about your birth family?

Do you know what Nutmeg remembers about living with Mummy Holly and Daddy Ginger?

Do you have a book that tells your story? Do you call it a life story book? Where do you keep it?

NUTMEG GETS A LITTLE SISTER: PRACTICE GUIDELINES

PAGES 14-17 One of the family

Most children quickly get used to having a new sister or brother and find it hard to remember being without them. However, there will be times when they wish the new baby was far away. Adopted children should feel that their views are heard and valued, but they must not believe that they can decide whether another child stays permanently any more than birth children can decide whether their parents should have a baby.

Is Pip one of the family now?

Do Nutmeg and Poppy and Hops want Pip to stay for always?

Do you think Pip understands about being adopted?

Is there anything you would like to say to Pip?

PAGES 18-21 Preparing for court

Adopted children like to hear about 'What happened when I was adopted?' just as other children might ask: 'Tell me about when I was born'. Nutmeg may remember the Wise Owl judge but Poppy and Hops were too young to understand what was going on. Getting ready for Pip's adoption and explaining the process will renew the whole family's awareness of their life-long commitment to each other.

"Practising" will make it fun and deal with any nervousness about going to court. Most judges will enter into the spirit of a family occasion, willingly posing for photographs and even allowing children to try on their wig.

Who went to court when Pip was adopted?

Nutmeg's best clothes are his striped scarf and smart jacket; what do you like wearing best?

Do you remember when you went to see the judge? Who came with you?

Did the judge look like a wise owl? Was it a man or a woman?

Did the judge say anything to you?

Do you think this is a special day for Pip?

PAGE 22 Adoption day

Many families mark the significance of adoption by celebrating adoption day every year, like an extra birthday. Nutmeg, Poppy, Hops and Pip might share an adoption day – perhaps in the middle of the summer holidays so that the whole family can go on a special outing. In the meantime Pip is having an adoption party to welcome her into the family for always.

Do you know any good games to play at an adoption party?

Do you have an adoption day as well as a birthday?

How about making up a special song about adoption? It could go something like this:
Happy adoption day,
Happy adoption day,
Happy adoption dear Nutmeg
For always we say.